KNIGHTS AND CASTLES

Siege

Laura Durman

ARCTURUS

This edition first published in 2012 by Arcturus Publishing

Distributed by Black Rabbit Books
P. O. Box 3263
Mankato
Minnesota MN 56002

Copyright © 2012 Arcturus Publishing Limited

Printed in China

Library of Congress Cataloging-in-Publication Data

Durman, Laura.
  Siege / by Laura Durman.
    p. cm. -- (Knights and castles)
  Includes index.
  Audience: Grades 4 to 6.
  ISBN 978-1-84858-562-1 (hbk. : library bound)
  1. Siege warfare--Juvenile literature. 2. Sieges--Juvenile literature. 3. Castles--Juvenile literature. I. Title.
  UG444.D87 2013
  355.4'4--dc23
                              2011051446

Series Concept: Discovery Books Ltd.
www.discoverybooks.net
Editor for Discovery Books: Laura Durman
Designer: Ian Winton

Picture credits: Château des Baux de Provence http://chateau-baux-provence.com: cover and p 5, pp 8 (www.topphoto.fr.com), 9 (ARMEDIEVAL / www.topphoto.fr.com), 10t (Culturespaces); Corbis: pp 7 (Adam Woolfitt / Robert Harding World Imagery), 23 (Alfredo Dagli Orti / The Art Archive), 24 (Alfredo Dagli Orti / The Art Archive); Peter Dennis: pp 11, 22, 28; Getty Images: pp 10b (Dorling Kindersley), 12 (Ira Block), 16b (Leemage); Shutterstock Images: pp 4 (TimBurgess), 6 (PLRANG), 13 (Iakov Filimonov), 14t (Marcel Jancovic), 14b (holbox), 15 (Sergey Kamshylin), 16t (Nick Jay), 17 (aislin), 18 (MikeNG), 19 (Jaime Pharr), 20 (p_a_p_a), 21 (Sergey Kamshylin), 25 (roger pilkington), 27 (fdimeo), 29 (Boris Stroujko); Wikimedia Commons: 26t, 26b (Eugene Viollet-le-Duc).

Every attempt has been made to clear copyright. Should there be any inadvertent omission, please apply to the publisher for rectification.

SL002133US
Supplier 03, Date 0412, Print run 1457

Contents

Under attack

During the **Middle Ages**, powerful kings and lords built castles across Europe. During a siege, a lord tried to take control of another's land by capturing his castle.

The besieging lord and his army would surround the castle and cut off its supplies, leaving the defenders to starve. They would then wait for the castle's lord or **constable** to **surrender**. However, the longer a siege lasted, the more expensive it became. So if the **inhabitants** refused to surrender, the army attacked the castle and tried to overrun it.

A prolonged siege of Donnington Castle, in southern England, lasted from July 1644 to April 1646. Today only this twin-towered gateway remains.

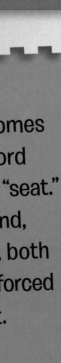

Take a seat

The word "siege" comes from the French word *siège* which means "seat." Sieges were long and, without surrender, both sides were forced to sit it out.

Besieging forces tried to break into the castle using a variety of methods. They might use ladders to climb over the walls or use a battering ram to break through the front door. They also pounded the walls with boulders fired through the air by large siege machines (see pages 8–11).

In this siege **reenactment**, soldiers scale the walls of Château des Baux, in France, using ladders. Castle defenders often used forked sticks to push ladders away from the walls during a siege.

SUMMER SIEGES

Many sieges took place in late summer. At this time of year, the fields surrounding a castle were full of crops. This provided food for the attacking army.

Plan of attack

Sieges were extremely expensive and often lasted a long time. The attacking army used lots of different tactics to try and force the castle dwellers to surrender as quickly as possible.

Once the castle was surrounded, the attackers would offer a **truce** or settlement. While this was being considered, the besieging army would work on a plan of attack in case the castle refused.

The attacking lord would gather his forces outside the castle in an attempt to intimidate those inside. The best possible outcome for the attackers was if the castle surrendered quickly.

Run away!

Powerful lords were sometimes able to summon large forces to help them fight off the attackers and keep control of the castle. In these cases, the besieging army could be forced to **retreat**.

The attackers would identify the weakest points of the castle and decide how best to destroy them. If there was no sign of surrender, the attacking lord would send his carpenters and blacksmiths to build huge siege machines. Then the battle commenced.

As well as attacking the outside of the castle, clever enemies mined underneath it. Tunnels held up by wooden props were dug under castle walls and towers. Once the tunnel was complete, the props were set alight. The fire caused the tunnel to collapse, often taking part of the castle with it.

Castles such as Beaumaris Castle in Anglesey, Wales, were designed to combat undermining. If miners managed to breach the outer wall, a second inner wall stopped the army invading the castle. Soldiers trapped between the two walls could easily be shot at by archers.

RUBBLE TROUBLE
When tunnels were dug under a castle, the rubble was often used to fill the **moat**. This meant that the enemy could easily walk up to the castle walls.

The trebuchet

The trebuchet was a large siege machine. It was used to hurl huge rocks at a castle to smash down the walls. The trebuchet was a very accurate weapon made by expert builders and designers.

The trebuchet was so accurate that it could be used to hit the same patch of wall repeatedly during a siege.

Ballast box

Throwing arm

Wheel

Sling

The trebuchet had a long throwing arm. At one end was a sling and at the other was a large, heavy weight called the ballast box. Men turned the trebuchet's wheels to pull back the throwing arm and raise the ballast box into the air. The arm was then held in place by a latch. Once the sling was loaded with **ammunition**, the latch was released. The ballast box fell very quickly and the throwing arm was flung into the air. This sent the ammunition flying at the castle walls.

AWFUL AMMUNITION

Sometimes attacking armies would fire rotting animal carcasses into the castle using the trebuchet. They hoped that they would spread disease and force the castle inhabitants to surrender.

The trebuchet was capable of throwing 200-pound (90 kg) stones as far as 1,000 feet (300 m). As well as battering the walls, the trebuchet could be used to launch missiles over the castle walls, causing damage and injury inside.

Soldiers work hard to turn the trebuchet's wheel.

Other siege machines

Several other large machines were used during siege warfare, as well as the trebuchet. Seeing these machines approaching would have struck fear in the hearts of the castle's **garrison.**

The mangonel was a different type of catapult. It could fire rocks farther than the trebuchet–about 1,300 feet (400 m)–but not very high off the ground. It had a long arm that ended in a bowl-shaped bucket. The bucket was loaded with ammunition and then the arm was released.

Arm

Missiles were launched from the mangonel's giant arm, which looked a bit like a spoon.

Battering rams were used to smash through castle walls and doors. The ram itself was usually a tree trunk. It hung inside a triangular wooden structure that protected the soldiers inside from the defenders' arrows.

Soldiers use a battering ram to smash through the castle **portcullis** and gate. The roof of the wooden shelter (cut away here to show inside) is covered in animal hides to protect it from flaming arrows fired by castle defenders.

Softening the blow

Some castles lowered a large pad or mattress in front of a battering ram to muffle its blows. Others lowered an object called a grappling iron to try to trap the ram and stop it from swinging.

The belfry was a huge wooden tower that was as tall as (or even taller than) the castle walls. The tower had a staircase inside so that troops were protected by the walls as they climbed up.

The platform at the top had a wooden **drawbridge**. Once the tower had been wheeled up to the wall, the drawbridge was lowered and the attacking soldiers spilled out into the castle.

Belfry

Mangonel

Trebuchet

This army is using a variety of siege machines to attack a castle, including a belfry containing a battering ram. Defenders fire arrows from the castle walls.

Weapons at hand

As well as the large machines, smaller weapons were also used during a siege. Arrows and **bolts** were fired by both sides. Knights and soldiers carried swords, spears, and **pikes** to fight off enemies who made it onto, or over, the castle walls.

Longbows and crossbows were popular weapons among castle defenders. The crossbow fired bolts with a lot more force than the longbow's arrows. However, it took a while to load a crossbow. Only two bolts could be fired each minute, whereas a strong bowman could fire 12 arrows in the same amount of time from a longbow.

A soldier keeps an eye on approaching attackers as he prepares to fire his crossbow.

Medieval swords were made from a mixture of iron and steel. They were tough and **flexible** with hard cutting edges. Many soldiers also carried a dagger, which could be used to stab between the joints of an **opponent's** armor.

During peacetime, the castle's soldiers would practice their swordfighting skills with each other.

Many other weapons were also used such as axes and maces. The mace had a heavy steel head attached to a wooden handle. It could be used to deliver powerful blows, sometimes even breaking through a soldier's armor.

Personal protection

Knights and soldiers wore metal armor to protect themselves. Different types of armor developed over the centuries as weapons became increasingly deadly.

This early medieval soldier wears a chain-mail hauberk and hood as well as mittens to protect his hands.

The soldiers in early castles wore chain-mail tunics called hauberks. This flexible armor was made from thousands of tiny iron rings linked together. Early hauberks had a hood and reached down to the man's elbows and knees. The sleeves became longer in the 12th century, and chain-mail leggings were often worn under the hauberk by then, too.

From the late 13th century, chain mail was replaced by plate armor. The plates were usually made from steel, although sometimes leather or whalebone was used. The plates could be joined together to create a full suit of armor.

The plates of a knight's suit of armor were either jointed or held together by leather straps or rivets.

A knight could not put his armor on himself. His **squire** carefully strapped each plate of armor into place from the feet upward until the suit was complete.

It was very important for soldiers to protect their heads during battle. Early helmets were domed and featured a nose guard. Square helmets, called helms, later became popular. However, it was difficult to see through the narrow slit at the front of these helmets and they were very hot to wear. The helm was eventually replaced by the basinet, which had a pointed visor at the front. Raising the visor allowed soldiers to keep cool and see clearly.

This soldier wears an open-faced helmet called the basinet. The visor could be lowered to protect the face during battle.

15

Pr paring for a siege

Surprise attacks on castles were rare, so the lord and his garrison often had time to prepare for a siege. These early preparations could make the difference between winning and losing the battle.

Upon hearing of a likely attack, the first thing the lord did was to summon his loyal knights. They arrived at the castle armed and ready to protect the lord and his family.

A knight arrives at the castle ready to defend his lord.

The next most important thing was to gather as much food as possible inside the castle. Sieges could last months, even years, and those living inside the castle would have to survive on the food stored within.

The more food and drink collected in preparation for a siege, the longer the castle hoped to hold out against their enemy.

While the food was being collected, workers extended the castle walls with wooden **hoardings**. These protected both the defenders and the walls. Animal hides were then nailed to the hoardings to shield the wood from flaming arrows.

Once all of the food had been collected and everyone was inside the castle, the gates were closed and the heavy portcullis was lowered. Finally the drawbridge was raised. This meant that the attackers would have to find a way over the moat before reaching the castle.

Once the portcullis was lowered and the drawbridge was raised, the entrance to Hever Castle in Kent, England, was protected by the deep, water-filled moat.

Portcullis

Drawbridge

DON'T BE FOOLED!

Defending armies often placed stuffed dummies on top of the battlements to make the enemy think that the castle was heavily protected.

Castle defenses

Castles were towering fortresses that were built to protect the lord and his family. The castle's location and many of its features were designed to help the garrison fight off attackers during a siege.

Most castles were built high on a hill or a cliff. This meant that enemies could be seen from a good distance. To attack the castle, they had to climb up the steep slope while the defending army showered them with arrows.

Building a stronghold high up on a mountain or cliff meant that an approaching army could be seen long before it reached the castle. This gave the inhabitants plenty of warning of a possible attack.

Castle walls were very thick—usually more than 8 feet (2.5 m). This made them extremely strong and difficult to smash through. Wooden hoardings, however, could easily be damaged by flying rocks. They were later replaced with stone versions called machicolations.

At the top of the castle walls were **crenellations**. These provided gaps (crenels) through which the archers could fire at the invaders, and solid sections (merlons) to shelter behind while they reloaded. The walls also contained slits called arrow loops. The loops were wider on the inside so that archers could take careful aim, but narrow on the outside so that attackers could not fire into the castle.

This photograph shows the view looking out through an arrow loop. The gap on the inside is much wider than the slit on the outside. You can also see how thick this castle wall is.

Besieging armies would fire flaming arrows at the castle, or launch barrels of burning tar from their siege machines. To combat this, wealthy lords replaced their **thatch** with roofs made from fireproof materials, such as lead or slate.

FIRE EXTINGUISHER
During a siege at Exeter Castle in 1136 the garrison used wine to extinguish fires, due to a shortage of water.

19

The garrison

The lord employed a garrison of men to defend the castle. These soldiers lived in the castle and performed their duties under the command of the constable.

The men-at-arms were trained to fight with different weapons. Some were archers, using longbows or crossbows, and others were expert sword fighters. Of course, during a battle, they would use whichever weapon came to hand!

The garrison was employed to protect the castle during a siege. Ferocious hand-to-hand combat would take place once an enemy breached the castle walls.

Watchmen kept a permanent watch from the castle towers. They checked on the enemy's progress and kept an eye out for new forms of attack. If the lord left the castle, watchmen sometimes acted as his personal bodyguards.

INSIDE INFORMATION

Some garrison members, such as watchmen, were given very low wages. It was, therefore, quite common for soldiers to be **bribed** to act as spies for the besieging army. They would send out useful information, such as details of weak points within the castle.

Knights often owned manors on the lord's land and were, therefore, **bound** to protect him and his castle during a siege.

Pages and squires were young boys who were studying to become knights. Pages would probably not have become involved in fighting during a siege. However, in desperate times, squires might be called into battle. They were trained to fight with swords and also looked after the knights' weapons and armor.

A young squire practices his sword-fighting skills. He hopes to become a knight one day.

Defense tactics

Whether you were attacking or defending a castle, there were advantages and disadvantages on both sides. The garrison had a host of defensive tactics up their sleeves to keep the enemy out.

Archers inside the castle constantly peppered the attackers with arrows. Blacksmiths and **fletchers** worked tirelessly to keep the archers supplied with arrows and bolts.

The battlements had several holes in the floor, known as murder holes. Boiling water, hot sand, and **quicklime** were poured through the holes on to the attackers below.

Red-hot sand, poured through a castle's murder holes, could **penetrate** the joints of armor and cause serious injury to an attacker.

The garrison placed bowls of water on the floor. If ripples appeared, it was likely that the attackers were mining below the castle walls. The garrison might dig a counter tunnel and attack the unsuspecting miners underground. Or they might lower pots of burning sulfur to fill the tunnel with smoke.

FOOD FIGHT

Sometimes defending armies **pelted** their enemies with bread. This implied that the castle was so well stocked with food that it could survive an extremely long siege.

Castle defenders would pelt enemies with stones, and sometimes even with food. Castle walls were often sloped at the bottom so that objects thrown from above would bounce off and hit attackers.

The garrison also mounted surprise attacks, called sorties, on the enemy at any opportunity. Sorties often took place at night. A small number of soldiers would sneak out of a hidden entrance in the castle and attempt to catch the enemy off guard. They might try to destroy a siege machine or set the enemy's camp on fire.

Surrendering

Sieges could last for a long time with neither side succeeding in defeating the other. More often than not, sieges ended in a formal agreement or peace **treaty**.

The castle's lord or constable was often given between 7 and 40 days to consider surrender before the fighting started. During this time, castle dwellers could leave unharmed, carrying their personal possessions and weapons.

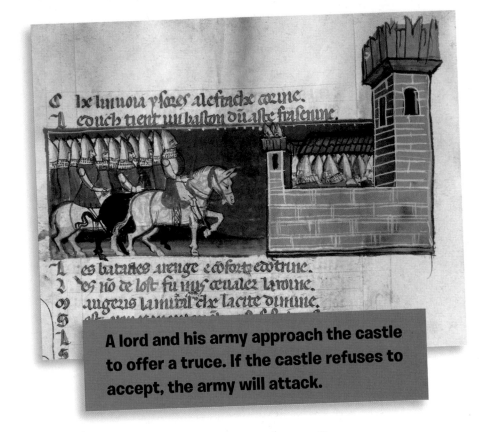

A lord and his army approach the castle to offer a truce. If the castle refuses to accept, the army will attack.

Should the castle refuse to surrender, battle would commence. The attackers signaled the start of the siege with flags or by launching missiles at the castle. From this point, the inhabitants ran the risk of being killed by the invaders when the castle was finally taken.

I surrender!

As food supplies ran short during a siege, women and children became an increasing burden. Although they ate the provisions, they could not help to defend the castle. So they were often encouraged to leave the castle while the offer of surrender was being considered.

Castles often surrendered due to lack of food or because disease had broken out. Another common reason was simply boredom. Life inside the castle became increasingly uncomfortable over time, and the besieging army cut off all contact with the outside world.

In 1300 Caerlaverock Castle in Scotland became a target for the King of England, Edward I. He approached the castle with 87 knights and 3,000 soldiers. The castle garrison, made up of only 60 men, put up a brave fight, but was eventually forced to surrender.

DISASTROUS DISEASE

A siege took place at Kenilworth Castle, England, in 1266. After six months the inhabitants were forced to surrender, due to an illness called **dysentery**.

In the 12th century, English King Richard I built a castle called Château Gaillard. It overlooked the River Seine in France. In 1203 the castle was besieged by the French under the command of King Philip II.

King Richard I of England and King Philip II of France were fierce rivals. Here they face each other in battle in 1198, five years before Philip besieged Château Gaillard.

Built high on a cliff and surrounded by a deep ditch, Château Gaillard could only be attacked from one side. It had three different sets of **fortifications** that a besieging army would have to overcome.

King Philip's forces waited for seven months, but the castle refused to surrender. So they then began to undermine the wall of the outer court. A fire was lit in the finished tunnel and eventually the wall collapsed. The defenders retreated to the middle court.

Outer court

Middle court

Moat

Inner court

This plan shows the three sets of fortifications that King Richard designed for his castle.

The besiegers were faced with another strong castle wall. They searched for a weak point and were lucky. The chapel was poorly protected and a soldier managed to break into it through a window. He then lowered the drawbridge to let his comrades in.

The castle's garrison retreated to the inner court. Surrounded by a moat, this part of the castle was reached by a natural rock bridge. The attacking army used the bridge as shelter from the defenders' bolts and arrows as they mined under the third wall. The wall was eventually breached, and the siege finally ended.

DIRTY TRICK

Many reports tell that Philip's army broke through the second wall by climbing a **garderobe** shaft. Historians believe this story was made up by the French to avoid admitting that they broke into the holy chapel.

The ruins of Château Gaillard can still be seen today. King Richard believed that the castle, built on top of a cliff, would be strong enough to keep his enemies out.

Changing times

The use of gunpowder spread through Europe in the 14th and 15th centuries. This movement signaled the end of siege warfare and, to some extent, the need for castles.

The first cannons were very unreliable and the soldiers who loaded them were regularly killed by accidental explosions. However, by the mid-1400s, the cannon had become a deadly weapon. Cannonballs were made from stone and carefully carved to fit the barrel. When fired, they could crash through even the thickest castle walls.

Cannons had become important weapons for attacking castles by the middle of the 15th century.

Handguns also came into use during the late 14th century. These early guns had no trigger. The gunpowder had to be set alight with a slow-burning wick. Holes called gunports were cut into castle walls so that defenders could fire on approaching enemies.

Gunpowder and cannons meant that castles could be attacked without the need for long, expensive sieges or large armies. By the 16th century, castles were no longer seen as military fortresses that needed to be defended. Instead, they were often converted into grand homes. Several hundred years later, people began to build castles once again. However, these castles were inspired more by fairy tales than the need for fortified homes.

Stepping into a fairy tale

King Ludwig II of Bavaria built several beautiful fantasy castles during the 19th century. The most famous, Neuschwanstein, is said to have inspired the Walt Disney logo. Ludwig is sometimes referred to as "the fairy tale king."

Nineteenth-century castles, such as Neuschwanstein, were designed to be beautiful and show off their owner's wealth, rather than to be protective fortresses.

Glossary

ammunition objects that are fired from a weapon

bolt a short, heavy arrow that was shot from a crossbow

bound required to do something in exchange for something else

breach to break through something

bribe to pay someone in order to persuade them to do something for you

constable the person in charge of a castle when the lord was not there

crenellations low walls with gaps (crenels) and solid parts (merlons), also known as battlements

drawbridge a bridge that is hinged at one end so that it can be raised to prevent people crossing it

dysentery an illness that causes stomach pains and severe diarrhea

fletcher a person who made bows and arrows

flexible able to bend without breaking

fortification a building, wall, or ditch used to protect a castle

garderobe a medieval toilet

garrison a group of soldiers who defended the castle

hoardings wooden defenses built along the tops of the castle walls

inhabitants the people living inside a building

medieval describes the period of the Middle Ages in Europe from the 5th to the 15th centuries

Middle Ages the medieval period of history, between the 5th century and the 15th century

moat a deep, wide ditch surrounding a castle, often filled with water

opponent someone who is against you

pelt to throw something at somebody

penetrate to go into or through something

pike a very long spear that was more than 15 feet (4.5 m) long

portcullis a strong metal gate that was lowered to keep enemies out of a castle

quicklime a chemical substance that burns the skin

reenactment the acting out of an historical event

retreat to move away from an enemy who is more powerful than you

squire a boy between 14 and 21 years old who served and trained as a knight

surrender to stop fighting and agree that the other side has won

thatch roofing made from straw and reeds

treaty a formal agreement

truce an agreement between enemies to stop fighting

Further reading

Castle (DK Eyewitness) by Christopher Gravett (DK Children, 2008)

Castles (Medieval Warfare) by Deborah Murrell (World Almanac Library, 2008)

Castles Under Siege by Richard Dargie (PowerKids Press, 2008)

Middle Ages: Everyday Life by Walter Hazen (Good Year Books, 2005)

Siege! Can You Capture a Castle? by Julia Bruce (Enslow Publishers, 2009)

What Were Castles For? by Phil Roxbee Cox (Usborne, 2002)

A Year in a Castle by Rachel Coombs (Millbrook Press, 2009)

Web sites

http://www.castlewales.com/siege.html
Find out what happened during a siege and see photographs from reenactments.

http://www.medieval-siege-society.co.uk/Gallery.aspx
On the Medieval Siege Society web site you will find lots of images of siege reenactments.

http://www.middle-ages.org.uk/siege-weapons.htm
Read all about the siege weapons used to attack castles and how they were designed.

http://www.warwicksiege.com/
Find out about the siege machines at Warwick Castle. Fire a trebuchet at the castle in their interactive game.

Index